POPPEOPLE™

'N SYNC'S

Justin!

by Michael-Anne Johns

SCHOLASTIC INC.

New York   Toronto   London   Auckland   Sydney   Mexico City   New Delhi   Hong Kong

ISBN 0-439-22224-9

Designed by Peter Koblish

12 11 10 9 8 7 6 5   1 2 3 4 5 6/0
Printed in the U.S.A.
First Scholastic printing, October 2000

CONTENTS

iNTRODUCTiON

Justin Time

**"I started singing at the age of two.
If I could talk, I could sing."**

He is the undisputed hottest hottie going. While Justin Randall Timberlake may share lead singer duties with JC Chasez for 'N Sync, he stands front and center as this millennium's number-one heartthrob. Justin gets over 50,000 fan letters a month — more than his bandmates JC, Joey, Chris, and Lance. The other guys all admit Justin is hands down the best dancer in the group. And on top of that, in *Teen People*'s "21 Hottest Stars Under 21" 1999 issue, Justin got more votes than anyone else — he received thirty percent of the vote, just edging out the Backstreet Boys' Nick Carter, who got twenty-nine percent.

With all that going for him, it wouldn't be surprising if Justin was one big, walking swelled head. But Justin doesn't take all the accolades to heart. He thinks of himself as just one member of a boy band. "We don't pay attention to stuff like 'Who gets the most attention,'" he recently explained in an AOL on-line chat. "We have a nice group vibe."

Of course, the group *does* happen to be 'N Sync. You know, the boy band whose 1998 debut U.S. album, *'N Sync*, went "diamond" — in music-biz speak that means it sold more than *ten million copies*. And 'N Sync is the same group that stopped traffic in New York City on March 21, 2000, the day they released their second album, *No Strings Attached*, and made an appearance at the Virgin Records Megastore. And of course, *No Strings Attached* was number one on *Billboard*'s Top 200 Album chart the first week it was out; it sold 2.4 million CDs that debut week. It made history by breaking all first-week sales records ever (the previous record was held by Backstreet Boys' 1.1 million first-week sales for *Millennium*); and 'N Sync's multi-city summer 2000 tour sold out in less than an hour.

Justin Timberlake always believed in his band. He knew they'd hit it big even before the rest of the world had ever heard of five boys from Orlando, Florida, called 'N Sync.

CHAPTER 1

Just Justin

"Always strive to do your best, never give up."

At precisely 6:30 P.M., January 31, 1981, became a red-letter day for Lynn and Randy Timberlake. It was then that their beautiful blue-eyed baby boy, Justin, arrived. Who knew that the first wail of "baby Timberlake" would foretell the infant's future? Certainly not his parents.

Actually Lynn once said Justin was the *quietest* baby in the maternity ward of St. Jude Medical Center in Memphis, Tennessee. "When we first brought him home from the hospital," Lynn told *entertainmenteen* magazine, "he was the quietest little baby. He never cried, he was so good. Then at four months old, he was able to say mama. Since then, he's been talking and singing forever."

Many babies are attracted to the rhythm of music, but from very early on, it was obvious to Lynn and

3

Randy that Justin was musically gifted. Before he could even walk, he would keep time with music by tapping his feet. If Lynn and Randy played a fast tune, Justin's tiny toes would be wiggling with the beat. If they played a slow song, Justin's feet would slow down. Of course, music was always around the Timberlake household. Randy Timberlake sang with a bluegrass band. By the time Justin was three years old he would entertain everyone by harmonizing with his dad as he practiced with his group. Often, the little boy sang along with the radio.

"I've been singing since I was two," Justin told *Teen People*. "If I could talk, I could sing. I was [always] performing for somebody."

Justin's uncle, Jimmy Timberlake, agrees. During that *Teen People* interview, Jimmy observed, "Whether he was telling a joke or dancing in front of everybody at Christmas, Justin was always an entertainer."

A Star Is Born

Justin's childhood in Memphis was pretty typical. He was close with his family, had lots of friends, did well in school, and participated in extracurricular activities. From the time he could hold a basketball, it was obvious that he was a natural at sports. He even earned the nickname "Bounce" from his b-ball ability.

Justin gave his all to everything he did. Sometimes he may have pushed himself a little too hard. In her conversation with *entertainmenteen*, Lynn recalled, "Justin made his first B in third grade and it just crushed him. When he'd come home from school with a B, it was horrible for him. He was a perfectionist with school. He was so hard on himself, I told him, 'You know, it's cool. You don't have to be perfect all the time.'"

Justin's memories of his early years pretty much agree with his mom's. "I didn't get in trouble a lot," Justin told *SuperTeen*. "I'm not gonna necessarily say I was a good kid in school, but I was in good with all the teachers and principals. I never got in trouble."

However, if you dig a little deeper, Justin's halo slips just a bit. Justin's best friend from those early years is Trace Ayala. "We've been friends since we were born," Trace told *SuperTeen* magazine. "Our parents were best friends. . . . Justin and I went to elementary school together, and our families [still] go on vacations together all the time."

Trace's grade school memories differ just a little from Justin's. "We were always in trouble together —

not when we were separate," he says. "Not bad trouble — we'd just aggravate our teachers a lot."

What everyone agrees on was that he could *really* sing. Justin claims that from the time he was eight years old, he *knew* he was going to be a singer. "It just always felt natural to me," he told *Rolling Stone* magazine. Justin sang in the family's Baptist church choir and often performed in school productions. Once Justin and his buddies did a New Kids on the Block song-and-dance routine at a school assembly, and the kids — especially the girls — wouldn't stop cheering. Some girls even chased Justin and his friends down the hall — just like they were superstars! Little did anyone know that was a hint of what was to come years later!

Recognizing that Justin really had a gift, Lynn got him a vocal coach. By the time he was eleven years old, he was itching to take that big step toward being a professional singer. For Justin, that was trying out for the TV talent show *Star Search*.

"He just loved being onstage," Lynn told *Rolling Stone*. "He wanted to sing all the time. After he auditioned at the mall for *Star Search*, we went down to Orlando for the show."

Justin was picked for a segment of *Star Search*, and following in his dad's footsteps, he sang a country-western song. Tapes of that performance, which recently turned up on MTV, show little Justin wearing a huge cowboy hat and singing his little heart out. Though he didn't win the competition, he did walk away with the big prize: Justin was noticed by the producers of the Disney Channel TV show, *The New Mickey Mouse Club*, which had first hit the airwaves in 1989.

Over the entire run of the show, which was nicknamed *MMC*, some 30,000 kids auditioned. Eventually only twenty-one young talents were picked to sing, dance, and act in skits during the *MMC* years. At age twelve, Justin was chosen as one of the stars. For almost three years, Justin appeared on the popular show, now legendary for having produced future stars Christina Aguilera, Britney Spears, *Felicity*'s Keri Russell, *Young Hercules*' Ryan Gossling, and of course, JC Chasez. Though Justin was twelve and JC was almost seventeen, they became good friends.

Justin will never forget those *MMC* years. "I really started to find myself there," he told *Rolling Stone*. "It was a good experience."

Of course, life wasn't totally perfect for Justin. It was just around the time Justin got his Disney break that a different kind of break took place in his life. His parents split up. Justin and his mom moved to Orlando, and his dad, Randy, stayed back in Tennessee. Luckily,

Lynn and Randy handled their divorce carefully and as mature adults. They both loved Justin more than anything, and they didn't want him to have to choose between them. Even when Lynn later married Paul Harless and Randy wed his second wife, Lisa, Justin just felt that he got a bigger family. "I'm very fortunate to have the parents I do," Justin told *entertainmenteen*. "I call my stepdad my 'dad' and my natural dad my 'daddy.' Everyone is friends — everybody's cool with one another."

Justin's Good Luck Charms and Superstitions

1. Justin considers his gold necklace with his 'N Sync symbol his good luck charm.

2. "I used to have a lucky rock, but I lost it. So I was, like, 'You know what? I don't need it.' I guess I had to tell myself that after I lost it 'cause I wasn't going to find it again."

3. Justin has two lucky numbers. "Twenty-one or twenty-two. Twenty-one was my basketball number from middle school."

4. "When I'm in the car and I see an amber light at the traffic signal and we manage to get through it before it turns red, you must kiss your finger and touch the roof of the car to give yourself good luck," Justin told *Live & Kickin'*. "I've always done that."

5. "I'm cautious about silly little things like walking under ladders," Justin revealed to British mag *Top of the Pops*. "Even though in a way I don't believe in it, I kinda do believe at the same time. Say it's Friday the thirteenth and a black cat crosses your path. . . . It's spooky, isn't it?"

CHAPTER 2

The Mouse Ears and Years

"*The [New] Mickey Mouse Club* was the experience of a lifetime."

Justin got his Mouse ears — that is, he became an official cast member of *The New Mickey Mouse Club* — a few years after JC Chasez had joined the cast. So it was natural for JC to take Justin under his wing and show him the ropes.

JC still thinks about that time. Call it luck or fate or destiny, sometimes things seem to happen for a reason. JC marvels about the fickle finger of fate — and how his whole start in show biz might *not* have happened. "I landed a part in *The [New] Mickey Mouse Club*, but to be honest, I only went along to the audition to get out of going to school," he told *Live & Kickin'* magazine. "The weird thing is, if I hadn't skipped school that day, I'd have never met Justin and 'N Sync might never have happened."

The Mouse House

Being a "Mousketeer" was a lot of fun. At any given time during the show's seven-year run, there were twenty youngsters in the cast. The kids had the complete run of Disney World. But it was also a lot of hard work. It meant hours of dance and vocal lessons, rehearsals, tapings, press interviews, promotional appearances, as well as keeping up a full school schedule. Though each of the kids had at least one parent along at all times, many were homesick for the friends and family they'd left behind to work in Florida. That's one reason why, in spite of some large age differences, the "Mouseketeers" became very close with each other. It was like an extended family. They grew to know one another well.

Even so, today some of the former members of the cast admit to being surprised at how things turned out. Keri Russell, who is five years older than Justin, told *TV Guide* that she never would have guessed *he* would become so crushworthy — especially "seeing that Justin came up to my chest," she laughed.

Then there's Britney Spears. Though both Britney and Justin deny that they have been a steady couple for the past several years, it could be that a spark of romance started way back during the Mouse years. "Me and Justin," Britney told *TV Guide*, "we did duets together, and we would always eat lunch together in our dressing rooms."

During those lunches and times hanging out with each other, Justin, Britney, JC, and all the others talked about their futures. Even then Justin and JC shared a desire to belong to a singing group, and they often talked about the kind of music they wanted to perform. Those conversations may have been the seed that would eventually blossom into 'N Sync. Justin certainly credits those early days with JC as important. "Since me and JC were both on *The [New] Mickey Mouse Club*, I definitely think it helped with our music," he told one on-line fan in an AOL chat. "We got to sing a lot on the show."

Bye Bye Bye to Mickey

As they say, all good things must come to an end, and that was true for *The New Mickey Mouse Club*, too. The show ended in 1994, and the tight-knit group of "Mouseketeers" went their own ways. Justin was almost fourteen when the show was canceled. He remembers it was a big change. At first he and his mom, Lynn, returned to Tennessee. Justin went back to regular school and says he was "a kid for a second."

However, there was something missing, and Justin told *Teen People* he was *not* the happiest camper during that time: "I got so bored and really down about everything. I started to get a little rebellious. I didn't really get into trouble, but I wasn't focusing like I could. I didn't have the inspiration that music gave me, and it hit me: That's my place in the world. That's where I belong."

Horror Movies That Scare Justin Silly

1. *Urban Legend*
"I had nightmares about that movie. . . . The other day I saw a car with the lights off driving in front of me, and it was totally dark. I was, like, 'don't flash them, don't flash them.'"

2. *Scream*
"*Scream* startled me. That was one of those scary movies that, you know, there are scary movies that startle you for a moment and you laugh at them afterward."

3. *Silence of the Lambs*
"*Silence of the Lambs* scared me so much because [criminal profiling] is something you've heard about and you can relate to. It seems realistic and it could happen."

4. *Gremlins*
"When I was a kid, when I was really, really little, I saw *Gremlins* and I used to think that the gremlins lived under my bed — when I was like four or five."

5. *Nightmare on Elm Street*
"I always had this fear of my leg near the bed and having this arm reach out and grab my leg."

6. *Jaws*
"After I saw *Jaws*, I was, like, 'What's the point of going into the ocean?'"

CHAPTER 3

Justin Gets 'N Sync

"It was fate. Not a lot of people know what their love is before they're forty."

While Justin was home in Memphis and feeling itchy to get back to his first love of singing, things were happening back in Orlando. By the mid 1990s, Orlando had become a magnet for talented young teens. There were so many opportunities to break into show business there — Disney World, Universal Studios, TV and film productions, and a blossoming music industry. A young native of Clarion, Pennsylvania, named Chris Kirkpatrick decided to see what Orlando held for him. "When I was little, I wanted to be Gene Kelly," Chris once told *Teen People*. "He sang *and* danced." That was Chris's dream too.

So in 1990 he moved to Orlando and enrolled in college. There he joined the school choir and met another talented singer — his name was Howie Dorough. Even after they both left school, the two kept in touch. But that's jumping ahead.

'N Sync Is Born

Like many college students, Chris had to find a job to help pay for his living expenses. Never afraid of hard work, Chris landed several jobs. For a while he took photos of tourists at Sea World — or as he describes it, "annoying people." Chris, who had hoped to break into show biz down in Orlando, decided snapping tourist pics wasn't quite the road to success. He then joined a '50s doo-wop singing group at Universal Studios. But in the back of his mind, Chris always wanted to start his own group. So, in 1995, Chris put his plan into action. "I used to sing in coffee shops, and I decided to take it seriously and do this as a living," Chris told *Teen Beat*. "So, I called up a couple of my friends."

Actually, an agent in Orlando told Chris about Justin. When Chris called Justin in Memphis, he found out that JC Chasez was also there. It seems that after *MMC* was over, JC had moved to Los Angeles in hopes of landing a record deal. "I got hooked up with some slimy people and burned bad," JC told *Rolling Stone* for 'N Sync's *No Strings Attached* cover story. "Finally I got in my car and left." And on the way back east, JC stopped by Memphis and looked up his *MMC* pal, Justin Timberlake. They started writing some songs together.

They even made some demos in a Nashville recording studio. "It was fate," Justin says of their reunion.

However, Justin and JC weren't sure of the next step to take. JC had returned to his family's home in Bowie, Maryland, and started working as a waiter to save money. He planned to go back to Tennessee and work with Justin again.

The answer to "what next?" came when Chris called Justin, who in turn called JC. The three met back in Orlando and went about rounding out their fledgling group. When Chris had worked at Universal Studios, he had met singer/dancer Joey Fatone, Jr. Joey had been playing the role of Wolfman in the theme park's *Beetlejuice's Graveyard Revue*. They met up again when Chris, Justin, and JC ran into him at a Seventies Night at a club at Disney's Pleasure Island. The foursome clicked, and now the group had a solid basic lineup. "But we knew we still weren't complete," Chris told *TV Guide*, "because we needed a bass."

Trivia alert! There used to be another guy in 'N Sync — before Lance! Listen — first they rounded out the group with a guy named *Jason*! They began rehearsing. By this time, Chris was well aware that his old college bud, Howie Dorough, had joined a group called the Backstreet Boys who were already pumping up the volume in Europe. Chris took note of Backstreet's style — he liked it but didn't want to imitate it.

The Name Game

Things were going well, and it got to the point where the guys decided they needed a name. Actually, it was Justin's mom, Lynn, who came up with the name that would eventually be known all over the world. Lynn, who by this time had married Paul Harless, was living in Orlando. She sort of acted as "group mom" to the guys, and was often at rehearsals with them. According to 'N Sync legend, one day Lynn remarked how "in sync" the guys' harmonies were. Presto! That seemed like a perfect group name: In Sync. Then, one day when Lynn and Paul were out with the guys getting a bite to eat, Lynn started doodling on a piece of paper. Just fooling around, she began to arrange the guys' names and initials in different combinations. After lots of scribbles, Lynn realized that the last letter of each of the guys' names actually spelled 'N Sync!

Justi**N**

Chri**S**

Joe**Y**

Jaso**N**

J**C**

It was fate! Except that soon after, Jason left the group. That presented a little bit of a problem. Not only did he have to be replaced, they had to find someone whose first name ended in the last letter "N." Just kidding — that wasn't a requirement. Anyway, Justin called his vocal coach back home in Tennessee to see if *he* knew a bass singer who would fit in with the group. The vocal coach instantly recommended a young talent from Clinton, Mississippi. He was in a group called the Showstoppers and interestingly his *name* was Lance Bass. Okay, so his first name didn't end with an "N," but his last name summed it all up in one word! Lance couldn't believe it when the guys called and asked him to come to Orlando to audition. "I didn't think I'd ever get the chance to do something like this," he told *Rolling Stone*. "The opportunity is just not there in Mississippi."

When it was obvious that Lance fit like a glove, Lynn worked her magic once again, and nicknamed him "Lansten." 'N Sync had their bass and their "N."

Opportunity Knocks

'N Sync is very proud of their origins. They always make it clear that they were *never* the creation of some businessman or music company. "You'll never find an

ad in some old newspaper saying, 'Looking for a group,'"
Joey told *USA Today* newspaper. "We put this group
together ourselves. Chris got the idea, and he got ahold
of Justin, and Justin got ahold of JC, and that's how it
began."

It wasn't easy. There was little money, and the
guys all had to pitch together to make ends meet. They
really got to know one another back then. And Justin's
mom, Lynn, was everybody's surrogate mom.

In those days, JC recalls everything was share and
share alike for 'N Sync. "We lived together for a while,"
he told *Smash Hits* magazine about his days of sharing
a room with Justin. "He's not messy and he did the
housework."

However, Lance begged to differ with JC's opinion.
"Rubbish," he said. "His mom did it all. She cleaned his
room for him and everything! Ironed all his clothes . . .
everything!"

'N Sync's Unique

Chris is very proud of what he started. "I don't think
there's ever been a group like us," he told *Teen People*.
"There are groups like us . . . that you hear the vocals
and maybe they're lip-synching. There are groups like
us and you can tell they're singing live, but their show's

lacking [something]. We're the first group to throw in their face hard-core dancing and singing, then [slow up to] sing a pretty ballad, then [get] right back in their face dancing again."

In 1995 'N Sync decided to get the word out in the music industry that they were ready to go. In an interview with *Teen Beat*, JC recalled, "[We performed at] Pleasure Island, and we videotaped the whole thing. What we did was create a demo package. We sang some stuff in the studio, put it on a CD, and sent it out to all these different record companies."

In early 1996 the promo package landed on the desk of music manager Johnny Wright. Early in his career, he had been the road manager for the late 1980s teen sensation, New Kids on the Block. When Johnny moved to Orlando, he began managing local groups and hooked up with businessman Louis J. Pearlman. At the time, Mr. Pearlman was putting together the Backstreet Boys, backing them with his TransContinental Records company. While the Backstreet Boys were over in Europe getting their first taste of success, Mr. Pearlman suggested to Johnny that they look for another group to comanage and support. Johnny had just the answer — 'N Sync. He introduced them to Mr. Pearlman. Most of the guys had heard about Lou since he was making a name for himself in the Orlando music scene. Chris, of course, was more aware of Mr. Pearlman because of Howie being one of the Backstreet Boys. Still, it took 'N Sync a while to sign on with TransCon. Eventually they did, and within weeks of their initial agreement, they headed over to Europe to record and perform. Like the Backstreet Boys before them, 'N Sync went into the Stockholm studios of songwriters Max Martin and (the late) Denniz Pop. That recording session resulted in 'N Sync's first taste of mass hysteria. The girls in Germany, Sweden, England, even Hungary became huge 'N Sync fans. They were all singing "I Want You Back" and "Tearin' Up My Heart" along with the group at concerts and on the radio.

It was time for Justin, Chris, JC, Joey, and Lance to return home. It was as if the U.S. was singing "I Want You Back" to them!

CHAPTER 4

'N Sync: Part Two

"We want to be pioneers in the music industry. We want to make our own name."

It was 1998, and the Backstreet Boys had finally returned home to the U.S. from their "boot camp" years in Europe, Asia, and Canada. They were causing a major stir on the charts with their first U.S. CD, *Backstreet Boys*. It had taken them five years to hit the majors in America, but they were reaping the profit big-time.

'N Sync was nipping at their heels. With the same management and money team — Johnny Wright and Lou Pearlman — and basically the same songwriters and producers — Max Martin and Denniz Pop — 'N Sync was on the verge of breaking in America after only two and a half years in Europe. The Backstreet Boys were signed with Jive Records in the U.S.; 'N Sync went with RCA Records.

Clearly it was natural that critics and fans alike would compare the two groups. Though they knew one another and were, in fact, quite friendly, both bands were unhappy: According to some insiders, BSB felt that Johnny Wright and Lou Pearlman had created a "family" relationship with them and then made them feel like the stepkids when 'N Sync came along.

And 'N Sync didn't like being called the "kid brothers" of the Backstreet Boys. In *The Making of No Strings Attached,* Justin recalled, "When we put our group together — and we were together six months before we met Johnny — I didn't even know who the Backstreet Boys were."

And when reporters insisted on dwelling on the comparison, the guys were as diplomatic as possible — but firm. Justin told *Teen Beat* at the time, "I don't think we want to emulate anybody. We want to be pioneers in the music industry. We want to make our own name. We have inspirations individually and as a group. We look up to groups like Boyz II Men, Take 6, groups that really take time to do a cappella harmonies and those really tight intricate chords. But as far as being somebody, we want to be 'N Sync."

Back in the U.S.A.

'N Sync released their first U.S. CD, *'N Sync*, in March 1998. Though it was a modest hit, it wasn't a chart buster. Then, that summer, the Backstreet Boys had to back out of a Disney Channel concert. The Mouse House turned to 'N Sync and offered *them* the concert. They accepted and taped it in July 1998. "Even after we filmed it, we just thought it was a little concert," Chris told *Entertainment Weekly* magazine. "I was, like, 'Well, that was cool. Now we gotta go work on our careers.'"

But when the special ran on the Disney Channel in August 1998, things really began to heat up. *'N Sync* zoomed into the top ten on the album charts. The boys were recognized, chased, and deluged with mail from fans they never knew they had!

"I Want You Back," "Tearin' Up My Heart," and "Ain't No Stopping Us Now" all became chart toppers. The reaction was startling. Even 'N Sync's families were surprised by all the attention their sons were getting. Justin's stepdad, Paul, good-naturedly told *Teen Celebrity* magazine, "We weren't prepared for how energetic the fans would be. Lynn and I would sit down front, where we could see our son perform, and we had girls coming after us, telling us to get out of the way."

Not wanting to lose the momentum, RCA Records quickly sent 'N Sync back into the studio to record a Christmas CD. "Not just anybody can put out a Christmas album," JC said in *The Making of No Strings At-*

tached. "[You] have to have somewhat of a following for people to want to pick it up. And that made us feel very good."

It should have — the CD went multiplatinum.

However, little did 'N Sync realize it was going to be a long time before they felt so happy again.

Trouble in Paradise

By the beginning of 1999, fans had already heard about bad vibes between the Backstreet Boys and their management team. In fact, BSB had left Johnny Wright and Lou Pearlman and signed with another management company called The Firm. There were lawsuits, but most of the "inside stuff" stayed *out* of the headlines. When any of those involved were questioned about the split, they just commented that things were finally settled and everything was fine.

Meanwhile, 'N Sync was still promoting their first CD, which had by this time sold some ten million copies. They were also getting ready to go back into the studio to record their next album. After touring over the summer of 1999, 'N Sync was expected to release that album in the fall. It didn't happen. It seems that early in 1999, 'N Sync had decided not only to leave their record label, RCA, and sign with Jive Records (the home of the Backstreet Boys and Britney Spears) but also to split from Lou "Big Poppa" Pearlman. It became a very uncool situation. And a very public one. From September to December 1999, there seemed to be daily news bites on how "Pearlman had taken advantage of 'N Sync" or how "'N Sync was ungrateful for all Pearlman had done." It became a battle of lawyers. In the meantime, 'N Sync's new album, coincidentally named *No Strings Attached*, was sitting on a shelf, unable to be released until the legal problems were ironed out. It would take a lot of ironing, since Mr. Pearlman and TransCon Records sued 'N Sync for $150 million — and the boys turned around and filed a $25 million countersuit.

In an interview with *USA Today*, 'N Sync tried to explain their decision. Lance said, "At the end of every year, we evaluate everyone who works for us. And at that point in our career, [the people at] TransCon weren't doing anything for us."

"We felt like they were taking rather than giving," Justin added. "So we rearranged the situation."

In a more personal response, Justin told *TeenBeat* magazine: "The controversy is all hype. Our main concern has always been our music and getting it to our fans. That's what we're gonna do, no matter what it takes. We're gonna make sure our music gets to the fans because they showed us love on the first album and we're going to show them love on the second album. That's what we've always been about."

Indeed, 'N Sync took matters into their own hands. Reportedly, they worked on *No Strings Attached* even though they were up in the air business-wise. But that also gave them a certain freedom. Instead of having to accept producers, songwriters, and songs that record company executives normally chose for them, 'N Sync went out and worked with whomever they wanted. "We decided to do our new album independently," JC told *USA Today*. "We wanted to do it our way, from top to bottom. We chose every producer and every writer. When [it] started [coming] together, we didn't even *have* a record company!"

However, that also meant that there was *no* guarantee that any of the songs would end up on 'N Sync's next album — or if there would even *be* another 'N Sync album. (Part of the lawsuit against the group was the ownership and possible use of the very name 'N Sync!) However, that didn't seem to bother some of the music industry's biggest names. TLC's Lisa "Left Eye" Lopes, who rapped on "Space Cowboy"; mega-musicman Teddy Riley, who produced "Just Got Paid"; and songwriter/singer Richard Marx, who produced and arranged "This I Promise You" — all worked with the guys. The result, as everyone now knows, was the record-breaking album *No Strings Attached*.

Like his bandmates, Justin was extremely proud of *No Strings Attached*. In *The Making of No Strings Attached*, he explained, "We had more creative freedom this time. I think that when you listen to this album in comparison to our debut album, you'll say to yourself that we took our sound to the next level."

'N Sync gave their fans a taste of the album when they performed the first single, "Bye Bye Bye," on *The American Music Awards*.

Then, on March 21, 2000, 'N Sync proved to themselves and the rest of the world that they were their own men and not just some music mogul's puppets. That was the release date of *No Strings Attached*, and as Justin told *Rolling Stone*, "I think we really made history!"

CHAPTER 5

Justin on the Record

"Music is my life."

"Man, being onstage is like a different mind-set from anything else you've ever experienced," Justin once told *TeenBeat*. "It's like when you talk to an athlete, for instance, and you ask them, 'What were you thinking?' and they say, 'I was in the zone' — it's like that. You're just in the zone. I couldn't really explain the feeling when you're out before 22,000 people. I think that's how many [New York's Madison Square] Garden holds. You know, you can't really explain the feeling, muting everything you hear because it's so loud and the energy that flows."

According to Justin, *No Strings Attached* is the result of 'N Sync wanting to share that flow of energy with their fans. Even though the future of 'N Sync was up in the air when they recorded *No Strings Attached*, Justin says they felt like it was going to be their best work ever. "We said to ourselves, 'Well, right now, we are paying for this, so how do we get the producers that we want to produce our music? Just get them!'" he told MTV.

When they finally signed with Jive Records, 'N Sync brought them a near-finished product. Justin was thrilled when the record company loved what they had done. "They are so open to our ideas," Justin continued in his MTV interview. "They don't shoot 'em down. Even at the tip-top, [Jive CEO] Clive Calder is so hands-on with us in . . . this album. He's worked with us on it, and he's always asked us 'What do you wanna do?' And that . . . you can't beat that. When you have a record company that is behind you and works with you on your album, everybody's happy."

All in the Family

Justin is certainly very happy right now. He is doing *exactly* what he decided he wanted to do when he was eight years old. He's singing. And he's sharing his enthusiasm, his happiness, with millions of people all over the world.

He's also learned a lot about the music biz. So has his mom. When Justin was on *MMC* and during the early days of 'N Sync, his mom, Lynn, was always there. At first she was more like a den mother to a bunch of little cubs, but she quickly caught on to pitfalls that go hand-in-hand with showbiz kids. She was there when 'N Sync first hooked up, she was there when they signed their first label deals, and she was there when they toured all over the world.

By the time 'N Sync had come back to the U.S., Lynn had started her own artist management company. "It's called Just in Time Entertainment, named after Justin," she told *entertainmenteen*. "I am so fascinated by the business — you get sucked in being around all that creativity, you know? After helping the boys, I was, like, 'I can do this; this is my thing!'"

Today Lynn manages the Orlando-based all-girl group Innosence. They recently released their debut album and have toured with 'N Sync, Backstreet Boys, LFO, and C-Note.

Song by Song

Justin has branched out musically too. Both he and JC wrote or cowrote a number of the songs on *No Strings Attached*. Of course all the songs on the album have special meaning to the guys — but the tunes Justin contributed to definitely mean the most to him.

The following are some observations the guys made on some of *No Strings Attached*'s tracks.

"Bye Bye Bye": JC told *Disney Adventures*

magazine, "'Bye Bye Bye' is our way of stepping up, moving on, leaving the past behind and moving on to the future."

Right before they released that first single, Justin told *16* magazine: "People remember 'Bye Bye Bye.' It's a little more edgy, a little more R&B. You'll find us going closer to what we normally are used to on this second album and taking a bit more edge to our sound, which nobody's done. We want to be really innovative with this album, and that's what we're doing."

"Promise" and "Space Cowboy": "There's a song called 'Promise' that Richard Marx did," Lance told MTV. "It's my favorite ballad; then there's the song JC wrote called 'Space Cowboy.' It's all about the millennium. You've never heard this style of music. It's just funky and edgy. It's like a chant type song."

JC told *entertainmenteen* about his "Space Cowboy" song. "It's actually about the end of the world, believe it or not. It's about man's spirit to overcome. The whole song is about if the whole world comes to an end, what will we do? I say, we land on the moon. If the earth blows up, we still have the rest of the universe to conquer."

"Good for You": In *The Making of No Strings Attached,* Justin commented on the song he wrote. "It's about how I would treat a woman if I was in love with her. Like, 'I know the way I am is a bit overwhelming, but I want you to know that it's all from the heart.' That seems to be my problem with all my ex-girlfriends. I think I loved them too much from the beginning. I found out girls need to chase a little."

On the Road Again

There's little doubt that Justin is at an all-time high in his life. His career is soaring, he's writing and creating the music he loves, and though *he* won't officially comment on it, Britney Spears told *Rolling Stone* magazine that she and Justin "occasionally" cuddle up.

After all the professional unrest of the past year, Justin was really looking forward to bringing 'N Sync's new material to their fans. Just before 'N Sync geared up for their megacountry world tour for *No Strings Attached*, Justin could barely contain himself. "I love touring because it gives everybody a chance to see you doing what you love to do and it gives them a chance to relate the songs to the faces," he said in an on-line chat. "It gives [fans] a chance to see the show. . . . I think the coolest thing about what we do is getting to touch so many people with our music and the positive look that people get from our music. It's a great feeling to be part of that."

Giving Back

And Justin wants 'N Sync fans to have the chance to really share in the joy he gets from music — not just by listening to their CDs or going to their concerts. In the fall of 1999 he created the Justin Timberlake Foundation. Its main purpose is to give funding to public schools to help create music and art educational programs.

"I grew up in the boondocks, and there just wasn't a good musical program at school," Justin told *Rolling Stone* magazine. "I've thought about it a little bit — this and the whole Columbine incident. Music is another way for young minds and young bodies to express themselves, to find a way to get all those [sometimes] negative thoughts and energies out."

In October 1999 Justin was invited to Washington, D.C., to attend a conference on how to help others. It was hosted by the First Lady, Hillary Rodham Clinton, and as part of the day's activities Justin was invited to an elementary school. It was there he announced the creation and explained the mission of his foundation: "I know from my own experience that music gives kids a way to channel their energy and emotions into something positive.

"It's so important for kids to have the chance to find what they're good at in school and feel like they're part of the system, and music is something that can make that happen in a creative and exciting way."

Through the Justin Timberlake Foundation, he added, "I want to raise enough money to get things up to speed with technology and inspire kids to pursue music. They should have everything they need to really do it."

Justin himself is an inspiration for kids to use music as a creative way to express themselves. But in the real world, sometimes inspiration is not enough. Teachers, instruments, even computer musical programs cost money — lots of money. And Justin has been so blessed and so lucky to have found success in the field he loves, he wants to share that with his fans.

Justin's Jewelry

1. He alternates wearing the 'N Sync charm with the JTR pendant around his neck — he created the design around his initials. "It was a present from me to me," Justin told *Live & Kickin'* magazine. "It's a bit of a dagger and has loads of diamonds in it. I had it made with my initials. It was heavy to wear at first, but I'm used to it now." Justin has a tattoo duplicate of it on his right ankle.

2. Justin also wears a WWJD bracelet. The initials stand for "What Would Jesus Do?" "It's like a friendship bracelet, but more spiritual. I never take it off. By wearing this bracelet, I find it helps me think before I do something."

3. "I like gold and diamonds, but if I were gonna wear silver, I'd wear all silver. But if I were gonna wear gold, I'd wear all gold."

CHAPTER 6

Justin the Actor

"Music is definitely my first love, but I've always wanted to get into acting."

During 'N Sync's downtime (a nice way to describe the musical break they had to take while they were dealing with all their legal woes), Justin didn't sit back and relax. He wanted — no, make that he needed — to flex his creative muscles.

When he was in elementary school and junior high, he participated in a number of school musical productions and plays. And of course, he did skits on *MMC*. More recently, Justin made a guest appearance on ABC-TV's *Sabrina the Teenage Witch* and acted in the upcoming Lou Pearlman-produced movie *Jack of All Trades*. Though he has always considered himself first a singer, he is also a pretty good actor. And naturally, 'N Sync's fans get to see him play a role in videos like "I Drive Myself Crazy." So it wasn't so surprising that when Justin had some "free" time, he agreed to make his starring role acting debut in the ABC-TV movie *Model Behavior*, which aired on March 12, 2000.

Lights, Camera, Action

Model Behavior starred *Party of Five*'s Maggie Lawson, Kathie Lee Gifford, her son Cody Gifford, and Justin. Maggie played a teen supermodel named Janine who wanted to experience a normal teen lifestyle for a while. She traded places with a high school student — who just happened to be her exact double. Kathie Lee Gifford played Janine's mom, and Cody, her little brother.

Justin played Jason Sharp, another teen supermodel and friend of Janine's. Despite his last name, Jason wasn't "sharp" enough to realize that his friend had pulled a switcheroo. *Model Behavior* was a lighthearted comedy and not a huge challenge for Justin, but it was a perfect way to get his acting toes wet. Before Justin signed, however, he went to Chris, Lance, Joey, and JC and checked it out with them. "I got the blessing of the other four to do this [movie]," Justin told *Teen People*. "I would never do anything that they didn't approve of."

He was also totally up-front with the producers of *Model Behavior*. "I told them from the get-go, 'Look, I've done sketch comedy. I haven't done a lot of serious acting,'" Justin told *Entertainment Weekly*, adding, "It's a TV movie, it's not Shakespeare."

Though the movie was a comedy, Justin definitely took it seriously. He was determined to prove he was as much a professional on-screen as he is onstage. Michael Karz, executive producer of *Model Behavior*, told *Entertainment Weekly*, "[Justin] was nervous. But that made him perform even better. When we were shooting the movie [in Toronto], he never went out. All he did was stay at his hotel and go to the set."

Needless to say, Justin's appearance on the set did cause a stir with the female population of Toronto. Every day, there were crowds of girls outside trying to get a glimpse of the heartthrob. Surprisingly enough, that added to Justin's nervousness. When *TV Guide* visited the set, Justin candidly told their reporter, "If I were in the 'N Sync world right now, I'd feel more comfortable with the gawking and all the staring, but in this particular thing, I just try to block it out and do what I need to accomplish this."

If the crowds made Justin a bit jumpy, he tried not show it when he was in front of the cameras. Justin credits his *MMC* years with any self-confidence he has about acting. "It wasn't serious acting, but I got such good improvisational skills from doing sketch comedy," he continued in his conversation with *TV Guide*. "I don't feel too much pressure. Besides, that's how you accomplish things — you go out there and do it."

The Hard Part

Believe it or not, Justin admits that the most difficult part of his role was *not* memorizing his lines or putting himself in character — it was his first-ever on-screen kiss. He and Maggie Lawson had a smooch scene. Beforehand, Justin tried to act calm and cool as he discussed his upcoming liplock with *Teen People*. "It's not a big deal. As long as she's comfortable, then I'm comfortable. I just hope my breath doesn't stink!"

Always the joker, Justin seemed to be getting more and more at ease as the kissing-scene day approached. Once again he confided to the *TV Guide* reporter, "She [Maggie] doesn't know this yet, but I'm going to keep messing up so we have to do the kissing scene over and over again."

In the end, the scene went on without a hitch. "We nailed it right away," Justin confessed to *People* magazine, "so I didn't have to keep doing it."

So much for Justin's plan for multiple retakes!

Movie Stars

Of course, Justin's *Model Behavior* was a perfect rehearsal for a reported future 'N Sync project. According to the *No Strings Attached* cover story in *Rolling Stone*, there are *two* films being readied for Justin, JC, Chris, Lance, and Joey. In the article it was revealed that one project is a "big-screen rendition of Sid and Marty Kroft's *Bugaloos* and the other is a comedy in development by Tom Hanks's company, Playtone."

The plan has the guys in front of the movie cameras as soon as they finish their *No Strings Attached* tour, but the films won't be released before summer 2001 — probably later.

CHAPTER 7

Justin's Ultimate Stack of Stats and Facts

Justin's Personal Printout
Name: Justin Randall Timberlake
Birthdate: January 31, 1981
Birthplace: Memphis, TN
Childhood Home: Memphis, TN
Current Residence: Orlando, FL
Zodiac Sign: Aquarius
Height: 6' 0"
Weight: 155
Hair: Light brown — though he sometimes bleaches it
blond
Eyes: Blue
Personality: Charismatic, charming, sincere, and silly
Bad Habits: Justin says he "procrastinates and bites
his nails."

Parents: Mother, Lynn, and stepfather, Paul Harless; father, Randy, and stepmother, Lisa Timberlake

Siblings: Half brothers, Jonathan and Stephen

Nicknames: J Curly or Curly (because of his curly hair); Shot or Bounce (because of his love for basketball); the Baby (because he's the youngest in 'N Sync)

Pets: A cat named Alley; a cairn terrier dog named Ozzie

Phobias: He has an incredible fear of snakes.

School: Justin is a high school graduate who plans on attending college in the future.

Best Friend: Trace Ayala — they've known each other since they were babies.

Car: 2000 BMW M Roadster — it's a purple-blue two seater

Girlfriend: Justin continues to deny that his main squeeze is the lovely and talented Ms. Britney "Baby One More Time" Spears. They are, he allows, very good friends.

Musical Talents: In addition to his singing skills, Justin can play the guitar and piano.

First TV Show: Justin appeared on *The New Mickey Mouse Club* along with Britney Spears and fellow 'N Syncer JC, when he was twelve.

Childhood Hero: Michael Jordan

Collections: North Carolina University basketball gear (Michael Jordan went there); sneakers

Honors: 'N Sync have won the following awards:
- 1999 American Music Awards, Best New Group
- 1999 Nickelodeon Kids' Choice Awards, Best New Group
- 1999 Teen Choice Awards, Best Album

Fascinatin' Faves

Food: Italian — "I like pasta with meat in it. I like chicken Alfredo and bolognese sauces."

"Chef" Justin: He makes fettuccini Alfredo with crab meat.

Mama Lynn's Specialties: Chicken marinated in garlic, meat loaf and mashed potatoes, and pot roast

Ice Cream Brand: "It's made in Cincinnati — it's called Graeter's. It's the best."

Ice Cream Flavor: Baskin-Robbins daiquiri flavor — "That's my new favorite." (It used to be Ben & Jerry's chocolate chip cookie dough.)

Candy: "I like Runts. And my favorite candy is Sprees [especially the red ones]."

M&M's: Blue

Fast-Food Meal: "Wendy's Monterey Chicken Sandwich . . . if I go to McDonald's when everyone else wants to, I'll get a Quarter Pounder."

Drink: Milk

Cereal: "I eat a lot of cereal — Raisin Nut Bran, Apple Jacks, Oreo O's. But my all-time favorite, though, is the classic Cap'n Crunch. It's like a butter-honey-type cereal."

Type of Pizza: Pepperoni and cheese

Color: Baby blue — the North Carolina University basketball team color

Holiday: Christmas

Animal: Siberian husky dogs — "I just love the way they look and the fact that they have so much soft and silky fur."

Item of Clothing: Sneakers — he's got more than seventy pairs!

Clothing Stores: Abercrombie & Fitch, Champs Sports, Foot Locker

Boxers or Briefs: Boxer-briefs

Shoe Size: "Twelve or thirteen, depending on the shoe."

Hair-Care Product: TIGI Bed Head — "I take it everywhere with me. You just rub it on your hair and mess it up a bit."

Body Part: Hands

Sports: Basketball . . . "and football to play, and soccer to watch."

Beach Sport: Beach volleyball

Sports Team: Orlando Magic

NBA Player: Penny Hardaway

***South Park* Character:** Mr. Mackie, the guidance counselor — "I like his voice."

Vacation Spot: Hawaii

School Subject: Science

Pastimes: Basketball, relaxing, Rollerblading

Workout Exercise: Push-ups — Justin does 200 a day

Movies: *The Usual Suspects, Ferris Bueller's Day Off, Scream, The Matrix*

Board Game: Clue

TV Shows: *Seinfeld, Friends*

***Friends'* Characters:** Jennifer Aniston's Rachel and David Schwimmer's Ross

Author: John Grisham

Magazines: *Rolling Stone, Details*

Actors: Brad Pitt, Samuel L. Jackson

Actresses: Halle Berry, Tyra Banks, Sandra Bullock, Meg Ryan

Celebs He's Met: Janet Jackson and Will Smith

Music: R&B, rap

Musical Artists: Jimi Hendrix, Lauryn Hill, Stevie Wonder, Brian McKnight, Boyz II Men, Missy Elliott, Take 6

All-Time Best Song: "Every Stevie Wonder song —

Justin Randall Timberlake — he designed his signature necklace around his initials.

He's been making music since he was a kid — in his *Mickey Mouse Club* days, he sometimes sang backup for Christina Aguilera and Britney Spears.

Justin's megawatt smile is as bright as his diamond studs.

On the personal tip, as well as the musical vibe, this band's been "'n sync" with one another all the way — through good times and bad. Left to right: Lance, Joey, JC, Chris, and Justin.

Blendin' with fans in New York, Justin — that's a straw in his mouth — is all over video games. He plays to win.

What's up with the kerchief? It's either a fashion statement, or just covering up a bad hair day!

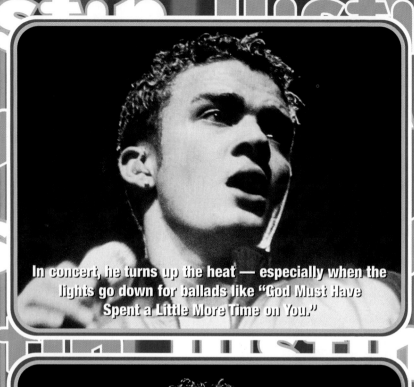

In concert, he turns up the heat — especially when the lights go down for ballads like "God Must Have Spent a Little More Time on You."

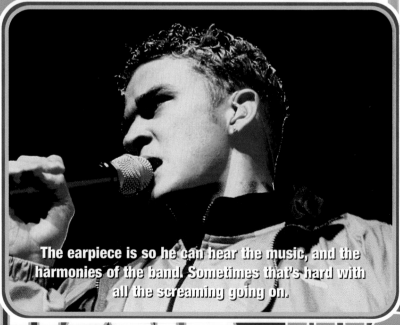

The earpiece is so he can hear the music, and the harmonies of the band. Sometimes that's hard with all the screaming going on.

Deep thoughts! "Always try to do your best, and never give up, no matter what." The best advice he ever got is what he passes on to friends.

'N Sync onstage — they sing "Bye, Bye, Bye," the fans go, "Hi, Hi, Hi!"

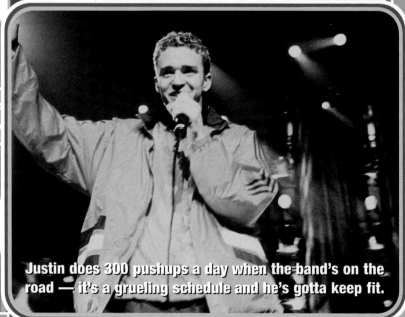

Justin does 300 pushups a day when the band's on the road — it's a grueling schedule and he's gotta keep fit.

He acted in the TV movie, *Model Behavior*, but music will always come first.

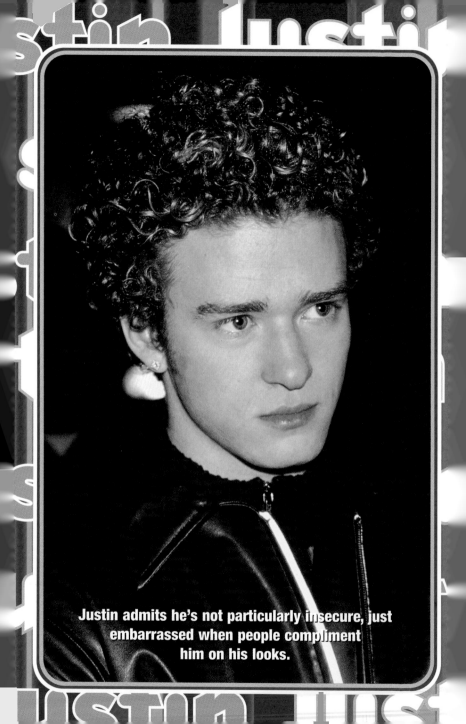

Justin admits he's not particularly insecure, just embarrassed when people compliment him on his looks.

"Food wimps," are the only kind of girls Justin doesn't like. "I like a girl who'll eat a [Burger King] Whopper with me," he once said.

What he'd change about himself if he could? His tendency to put things off instead of dealing right away.

He believes in angels.

Justin's tattoo — it matches the design of his necklace — is on his ankle.

'Ribbon in the Sky,' 'Ma Cherie Amour' . . . I could go on and on."

Song on *No Strings Attached*: "Promise"

Type of Girl He Likes: Intelligent

Super Power: To be able to fly

Theme Park Ride: Space Mountain at Walt Disney World

Childhood Possession: "I had a karaoke machine with a microphone and nobody could touch it except me. And if they did, there was trouble!"

Concert Medley to Perform: "The Jackson 5 medley — it's fun to dance to."

Fab Firsts

- **Toy:** A little plastic guitar
- **Concert:** The Eagles
- **Kiss:** "I was ten years old. I was in sixth grade and she was in eighth grade."
- **New Car He Bought Himself:** Ruby-red Mercedes-Benz M-Class
- **Pet:** "I was four or five — it was a dog and her name was Scooter. She was a mutt."
- **Celebrity Crush:** Drew Barrymore
- **Thing He Would Change About Himself:** His curly hair

Silly Secrets

- "I'm a sap when it comes to movies," Justin admitted to *YM* magazine. "I actually cried [when] I saw *Patch Adams*."
- "I used to have my hair cut into a shoulder-length bob and then have it shaved underneath," he confessed to *Live & Kickin'* magazine. "I much prefer the style I've got now though."
- When Britney Spears and Justin were members of *MMC*, they used to play Ping-Pong during taping breaks.
- Boys will be boys — "Everyone knows that I'm the best belcher in 'N Sync."
- Justin would like to meet actor Ryan Phillippe — "Everybody keeps telling me we look like twins."
- Justin was a straight-A student in school.
- Justin's biggest fears are "the three S's — spiders, snakes, and sharks."
- Justin says that if he were a cartoon character he would be Bugs Bunny because "he likes basketball, he likes Michael Jordan, he's pretty witty ... I'm pretty witty."
- Justin once dyed his hair baby blue! He and his best bud, Trace Ayala, used to love to dye their hair any color of the rainbow. "We used to dye our hair with Kool Aid!" Trace remembers.

- Justin likes to burn incense in his room, which is decorated in a "safari motif, with a Japanese screen and a big sleigh bed."
- Justin does a mean impression of MTV's funnyman, Tom Green.
- Each member of 'N Sync — including Justin — had his name engraved on a microchip (with about one million other names) that was placed in NASA's *Stardust* spacecraft. It was sent into space on February 6, 1999, and is expected to return to Earth in January 2006.
- As a kid, he used to practice singing by crooning along to Donny Osmond's old hit, "Puppy Love."

Instant Answers
Justin Takes a Personality Test

1. Confident or shy? "Confident. I feel I have an inner strength."

2. Romantic or cautious? "Romantic — when I fall in love, I go head over heels."

3. Competitive or laid-back? "Competitive — I like to win."

4. Moody or funny? "Funny. I joke around all the time."

5. Bee or wasp? "I'd probably rather be a bee. At least they're busy. And I'd attract people with my honey."

6. Gwyneth Paltrow or Cameron Diaz? "Gwyneth Paltrow, because I met her and she's hot."

7. *Dawson's Creek* or *Buffy the Vampire Slayer?* "*Dawson's*. I'm not too hot on *Buffy.*"

8. Crest or Colgate? "Colgate."

9. Ketchup or mustard? "Ketchup."

10. LA or NYC? "That's hard. Okay, New York."

CHAPTER 8

Justin Speaks — Outta the Mouth of a Babe

Is it hard being a role model for your fans?

"It's something that we didn't really ask for, but it's something that we realize has happened. We want our fans to know that we are human, that we do make mistakes."

Do you go to the gym?

"I don't have much of a chance to work out with 'N Sync's schedule . . . but I try to keep in shape. I do push-ups. People don't realize how productive push-ups are. You work out more than your chest. I like a lot of [exercises], just as long as [I] keep it even, I think you should work out every [part of the body]."

What were you like in junior high?

"I was a little bit of everything. I hung out with the girls a lot — I suppose I was a bit of a ladies' man, and I was on the basketball team, so I was a bit of a jock. I had the best of both worlds really."

Do you believe in angels?

"Yeah, I believe in angels. Seriously. That goes back to my religion. I believe there are signs everywhere. You can choose to deal with them or you can just ignore them, but I think they're always there. You can find out where your place in the world is, because I believe that everybody has the potential to make something happen in this world — to make a difference. I think angels are always there, watching over us. We picture them in a human form, but it's a spirit thing. I imagine them as a haze-type thing."

Is there anything you hate?

"Racism. To be judged or persecuted because of something that you have no control over — like the color of your skin or your religion — and to be outcast. . . . Racism is something that really, really bugs me. And it's sad, because racism is getting worse and worse. . . . but I think one day people are gonna realize how unimportant the color of your skin is."

Are 'N Sync and Backstreet Boys rivals?

"That's not part of my world. I'm not trying to be rude, but I don't have time to worry about some other group's problem. Do you know what I mean?

"We don't think about any other acts, whether they [are] boy bands or anybody else, when we try to do what we do. We're not here to compete with anybody. We're here to do good for ourselves."

Are the guys in 'N Sync *really* good friends?

"It may be hard to believe, but we are best friends. If one of us needs some space, then we give it to [him], but we love hanging out together."

What's it like to be famous?

"It's funny that people actually ask me for autographs. The main thing I want our fans to think about is that we are normal just like them. We like to do things just like them. We like to go to the movies just like them. We like to go shopping just like they do. I find it funny that they get into us as much as they do but I also find it flattering that they would take the time out to [listen] to our music."

Justin's Contact info Air . . . Snail . . . and E-mail

Record Company:
c/o Jive Records
137-139 West 25th
Street
New York, NY 10001
Official Website:
www.nsync.com
Official Fan Club:
'N Sync
P.O. Box 692109
Orlando, FL 32869-2109

Do you ever get depressed?

"There's definitely been times when I was totally depressed. But, you know, my spirituality helped me through that. I just feel like there's two of me: the public-eye me and the guy-who-brushes-his-teeth-twice-a-day me. They're getting along all right now. Sometimes brush-his-teeth doesn't get enough attention, but it's worth it."

Do you have a favorite vacation spot?

"Hawaii is the closest thing to heaven on earth that I've seen. I went there [a couple of] years ago and I had a fantastic time."

CHAPTER 9

Justin's Love-O-Scope

"I'm pretty honest, you know. If I'm interested in somebody, I'll just tell her."

'N Sync's hottie honey answers questions of the heart!

How do you deal with figuring out if a girl likes you just because you are famous?

"I'm pretty quiet [at] first. Instead of, like, talking and trying to figure her out, I kinda listen more. And somebody might get that impression about me, that I'm a little bit more quiet or, you know, a little bit more to myself. But that's because, when I meet someone, I kinda listen to what they have to say and then base my feelings upon that."

Would you kiss on the first date?

"I think that depends on the chemistry [between you and your date]. When you have chemistry with someone, you can usually tell right off the bat. I don't know if I'd kiss on the first date, though."

Were you in love with the first girl you kissed?

"I was nervous. I was with my girlfriend at that time. It was funny now that I look back at how nervous I was. I wouldn't call it love — I would call it an infatuation. I think when you're in love with somebody, you know it for sure."

Do you have crushes on any celebrities?

"Janet Jackson, Jennifer Lopez, Halle Berry, Tyra Banks — the list goes on and on."

Do you like to be asked out on a date or do you like doing the asking?

"I find it the best when it's just casual conversation and you come to [a] common ground and somebody in the conversation says, 'Hey, would you like to spend some time together?' You know, go out, and do something for fun or whatever."

Describe your dream girl.

"Confident, with a sense of humor. A good listener. Somebody with a sensitive heart. I am a hopeless romantic. I *don't* get off on people who make fun of other people. Somebody I could learn from, someone who would compliment me, someone who could help me grow as a person. . . . optimism — that's what I'm looking for. A little optimism in a world of sarcasm and pessimism."

What makes you notice a special girl?

"[Girls] who catch my eye . . . it all has to do with their attitude. If they're comfortable with themselves, it's easy to tell and that catches my attention. . . . Self-confidence. If you don't have [it], if you lack that self-confidence, it's hard for other people to be confident in you."

Do you know how to say "I love you" in any language other than English?

"In German — *Ich Liebe Dich.*"

What is the most romantic thing you've ever done or heard of someone doing?

"This isn't really for me — but my parents' [mom, Lynn, and stepdad, Paul] wedding anniversary is on Valentine's Day. How cheesy is that? I'm kidding — I think that's really romantic. I think my parents have really taught me how to be romantic."

What's your idea of a perfect date?

"I like doing spontaneous things — but it's kinda hard to do that on a first date because you don't really know each other very well yet. They don't know what to expect. If I was to say to somebody, 'Hey, I want to take her out on a date,' and I take her skydiving, she might think . . . [he laughs] . . . this guy is weird or something. . . . Sure, I'd take a girl skydiving.

Why not? It sounds like fun! Why not do something like that? The kind of ideas I come up with are spur of the moment, but they're not all wild. I also like having a quiet dinner at an Italian restaurant. A good conversation is cool to me. Then I can get to know the girl."

Have you ever had your heart broken?

"I've been left heartbroken many times. It's one of the worst feelings you can have. As far as me leaving someone else heartbroken, I can't say for sure. I hope I've never broken any hearts."

How do you get over a broken heart?

"Nothing helps except time."

Do you fall in love easily?

"No, but when I give [my heart], it's with a willingness that's sometimes overwhelming."

Justin Tattle-tales on Joey, Chris, JC, and Lance

On Joey:
* "Joey is [messy] — in more than one way. . . . [And] he's the most flirtatious person I've ever known."
On Chris:
* "He's really hyper, but it's not really a pet peeve. I think he's funny when he's hyper."
On JC:
* "JC always comes into a conversation in the middle [of it] and asks a question that was asked, like, five minutes ago — he does that every time."
* "JC doesn't even chew — he just tips the plate back in his mouth. This is no exaggeration!"
On Lance:
* "When we try to get [our ritual] hackey sack game when we're going onstage, Lance is a little too serious."

What turns you off about a girl?

"I don't like insecurity and jealousy. Sometimes with teenage romance, people try to get to know the other person before they get to know themselves. You start dating someone and start acting like someone you're not. I want a girl who knows herself and is comfortable with herself."

Is it hard to keep a relationship going while you are on the road with 'N Sync?

"It is hard but I'm convinced that it's possible to build something with somebody no matter how busy you are. If you really want to put the effort into a relationship, you will. It's just a question of organizing your time in the right way!"

How do you know you are really in love with the girl you are with?

"When she's the first thought in your head when you wake up and the last thought before you go to sleep."

Okay, the ultimate question — are you really dating Britney Spears?

"Things have gotten a little out of hand with my personal life being in the tabloids. So from now on I don't comment on who I'm dating. . . . I could have said yes and I could have said no, but it doesn't matter what you say because it still gets blown out of proportion anyway."

But, are you dating Britney?

"Britney is a good friend. I've known her since I was twelve. I choose to hang with people who are down-to-earth and very humble, and she's definitely one of them."

Well, are you dating *anyone*?

"I'm dating. It's hard to find people to date, period, without it getting blasted all over the tabloids. If someone comes along that I fall in love with, then I'm not going to be able to help it, and I'll be happy to show that to the world."

CHAPTER 10

How Well Do You Know Justin?

Are you Justin's Number One Fan? Do you know *everything* there is to know about him? Why not test your Justin-IQ with the following tasty tidbits of trivia?

True or False

1.) Justin was named one of *Teen People*'s "25 Hottest Stars Under 25" in the May 2000 issue.

True _____   False _____

2.) Justin got a speeding ticket in Florida shortly after he got his new BMW M roadster.

True _____   False _____

3.) Justin and the rest of 'N Sync announced they would be producing a musical feature film at Robert Redford's Sundance Film Festival.

True _____   False _____

4.) Justin hasn't been able to earn his high school degree because he's been too busy with his career.

True _____   False _____

5.) Justin has signed on to star in the sequel to the film *Dirty Dancing*.

True _____   False _____

6.) Justin spends more time in front of the mirror than any of the other guys in 'N Sync.

True _____   False _____

7.) 'N Sync's *No Strings Attached* sold 1.13 million copies on March 21, 2000 — the first day it was in the record stores.

True _____   False _____

8.) Justin sings the alto part in 'N Sync's harmonies.

True _____   False _____

9.) Justin is really very shy.

True _____   False _____

10.) Justin never drinks water!

True _____   False _____

11.) Justin wrote the song "I'll Be Good for You."

True _____   False _____

12.) Justin revealed that Joey is a real fan of Broadway musicals.

True _____   False _____

13.) Justin is a total loss in the kitchen — he can't even boil water!

True _____ False _____

14.) Justin appeared on the popular ABC-TV series *Who Wants to be a Millionaire*.

True _____ False _____

15.) Justin says he loved science when he was in school, but his worst subject was math.

True _____ False _____

16.) Justin recently revealed he was going to have his nose pierced.

True _____ False _____

17.) Justin once tried to iron his curly hair straight.

True _____ False _____

18.) As a kid, Justin used to go to summer basketball camp.

True _____ False _____

19.) One time when they were in Toronto, Canada, Justin, Lance, Joey, and JC all got a flame tattoo to symbolize their 'N Sync success.

True _____ False _____

20.) Justin admits that his worst habit is burping!

True _____ False _____

Multiple Choice

1.) One time Justin's luggage got lost and he had to borrow shoes and clothes. Who was the Good Samaritan?

a) Manager Johnny Wright

b) Lance Bass

c) Chris Kirkpatrick

d) JC Chasez

2.) What is the most important quality Justin looks for in a girl?

a) Beauty

b) Wealth

c) Confidence

d) Celebrity friends

3.) Justin's name in the ABC-TV movie *Model Behavior* was:

a) Justin Blank

b) Jason Sharp

c) Cody Dull

d) Joshua Fatone, Jr.

4.) Justin's favorite info site on the Internet is:

a) www.britneyspears.com

b) www.mrshowbiz.com

c) www.scholastic.com

d) www.rollingstone.com

5.) What is the main color in Justin's living room?

a) black

b) baby blue

c) white

d) red, white, and blue stripes

6.) Justin's astrological sign is Aquarius. What is the symbol for it?

a) A goat

b) A water carrier

c) Scales

d) A crab

7.) 'N Sync's first date for the *No Strings Attached* tour was May 9, 2000. What city did they play?

a) Orlando, FL

b) New York, NY

c) Washington, DC

d) Biloxi, MI

8.) The very first celebrity crush Justin had was:

a) Drew Barrymore

b) Annette Funicello

c) Meryl Streep

d) Brandy

9.) If Justin wasn't in show biz, what profession would he like to pursue?

a) Professional basketball player

b) Neurosurgeon

c) Farmer

d) Banker

10.) How many times a day does Justin brush his teeth?

a) one

b) four

c) two

d) every hour on the hour

11.) How does Justin mend a broken heart?

a) sleeps all day

b) isolates himself from everybody

c) listens to country music

d) eats ice cream

12.) In numerous magazine articles Justin has been described as a look-alike to what young movie star? (This is a bit hard, so we'll give you a hint — you might think this movie star is partial to Reese's Pieces candy.)

a) Freddie Prinze, Jr.

b) Leonardo DiCaprio

c) Seth Green

d) Ryan Phillippe

13.) Here's a little bit of a math teaser. In a previous chapter we listed how many *No Strings Attached* albums 'N Sync sold in its first week out. We also mentioned how many *Millennium* albums the Backstreet Boys sold in its first week on sale. If Britney Spears, who is on the Jive Record label, the same one as 'N Sync and BSB, sold 1.3 million *Oops! . . . I Did It Again* albums in its first week, how many albums did the three artists sell in their first weeks out combined?

a) 5 million albums

b) 100 million albums

c) 5.9 million albums

d) 4.8 million albums

14.) Justin told a newspaper columnist that he would like to trade places with someone for just one year. Who is it?

a) Kobe Bryant

b) Brad Pitt

c) Regis Philbin

d) President Clinton

15.) Who is the first person on Justin's speed dial on his cell phone?

a) Chris Kirkpatrick

b) JC Chasez

c) Lynn Harless

d) Christina Aguilera

16.) 'N Sync gets lots of presents from fans. What are Justin's favorite fan gifts?

a) Autographed pictures of themselves

b) Videos of fans performing like 'N Sync

c) Boxes of cereal

d) Coupons to McDonald's

17.) 'N Sync appeared at what major show biz awards show to sing "Music of the Heart" with Gloria Estefan?

a) The Grammys

b) The Soul Train Awards

c) The Golden Globes

d) The Oscars

18.) According to Chris Kirkpatrick, what is Justin's worst habit?

a) Forgetting things in hotel rooms

b) Forgetting the lyrics to their songs

c) Being late

d) Forgetting phone numbers

19.) Justin was born on January 31, 1981. What other member of 'N Sync shares his birth month?

a) Joey Fatone, Jr.

b) Chris Kirkpatrick

c) Lance Bass

d) JC Chasez

20.) Justin's siblings are:

a) Tyler and Heather

b) Molly, Kate, Emily, and Taylor

c) Steven and Janine

d) Jonathan and Steven

21.) Justin and JC were members of the Disney Channel TV show _The Mickey Mouse Club_. Which other member of 'N Sync met them on the set of the popular series?

a) Lance Bass

b) Joey Fatone, Jr.

c) Chris Kirkpatrick

22.) Daredevil Justin has tried this extreme sport:

a) Bungee jumping

b) Big game hunting

c) Mountain climbing

d) Snow blading

23.) Justin's favorite holiday is:

a) Fourth of July

b) Christmas

c) Presidents' Day

d) Easter

24.) What does Justin miss when he's away from home?

a) Running around barefoot in his house

b) Mowing the lawn

c) Walking his dog

d) Ordering pizza from Domino's

25.) What is the first store Justin would head for in the local mall?

a) Victoria's Secret

b) Mrs. Field's Cookies

c) Foot Locker

d) Pizza Hut

26.) Justin turns his nose up at what vegetable?

a) Broccoli

b) Spinach

c) Onions

d) Asparagus

Mix & Match

1.) Match each member of 'N Sync with his correct birthday.

Justin Timberlake ____

Lance Bass ____

Chris Kirkpatrick ____

Joey Fatone, Jr. ____

JC Chasez ____

a) January 28, 1977

b) August 8, 1976

c) October 17, 1971

d) January 31, 1981

e) May 7, 1979

2.) List these 'N Sync singles in the order of their release from first to last.

"God Must Have Spent a Little
More Time on You" ____

"Bye Bye Bye" ____

"I Want You Back" ____

"Tearin' Up My Heart" ____

"Merry Christmas, Happy Holidays" ____

a) first

b) second

c) third

d) fourth

e) fifth

3.) Identify each member of 'N Sync's correct middle name.

Randall ____

Scott ____

Anthony ____

Lance ____

Alan ____

a) Lance

b) JC

c) Justin

d) Chris

e) Joey

4. In the early days of 'N Sync, the guys gave each other nicknames. Match the correct nickname with each member.

Justin Timberlake ____

JC Chasez ____

Joey Fatone, Jr. ____

Chris Kirkpatrick ____

Lance Bass ____

a) "Big Daddy"

b) "Scoop"

c) "Lucky"

d) "Curly"

e) "Mr. Flirt"

Answers

True or False

1.) True: He was on the cover of the issue and even hosted the ABC TV Special, *Teen People's 25 Hottest Stars Under 25.*

2.) True: But Justin told *Teen People* he didn't try to get out of the ticket by asking the police officer if he wanted his autograph. "I was speeding, he caught me, and I learned my lesson," Justin said.

3.) False: They announced it at the Cannes Film Festival in France — they hope to start filming it in January of 2001, but it won't be biographical.

4.) False: Justin finished his high school studies — with honors — through the University of Nebraska-Lincoln independent studies program. He was surprised with his diploma when three of his tutors presented it to him at the 'N Sync concert in his hometown of Memphis, Tennessee. Justin celebrated it with 20,000 of the group's fans!

5.) False: Ricky Martin was tapped for the role — if the movie ever gets made!

6.) True: Chris told *Live & Kicking* magazine, "Justin — now he's got all that hair."

7.) True: They even beat the first day's sales record of the Backstreet Boys' *Millennium*.

8.) False: He shares the lead with JC Chasez.

9.) True: "I have issues meeting new people," he told *Entertainment Weekly* magazine, "because you wonder why they want to meet you."

10.) False: Justin told *Live & Kicking* magazine, "I drink eight bottles of water a day."

11.) True: "I actually wrote that song while we were doing our first headlining tour," Justin told *Wall of Sound* Internet news service. "I did it with the musical director of our band; we actually recorded a demo in a hotel room and originally didn't plan to use it for the group. But it ended up working out for the album, so that was cool. I wrote it to a would-be girlfriend; I can't say it was anybody in particular. I guess it's just how I would treat someone if I was, you know, madly in love with them."

12.) True: "He's really into Broadway musicals," Justin told *Smash Hits* magazine. "He knows lines from all sorts of shows."

13.) False: Justin has been known to whip up a batch of brownies every now and then.

14.) False: It was Lance Bass who joined *Millionaire* host Regis Philbin during Celebrity Week on the show. Also appearing were David Duchovny, Queen Latifah, Vanessa L. Williams, Rosie O'Donnell, Kathie Lee Gifford, chef Emeril Lagasse, Drew Carey, Dana Carvey, and Ray Romano.

15.) True: "I didn't like math that much," Justin told *Teen Beat*.

16.) False: Justin says on the Official 'N Sync Web site that he wouldn't pierce his nose — "It's dated."

17.) True: He told *Teen Power* magazine that he used a regular clothing iron and even burned off the ends of his hair!

18.) True: Justin told *entertainmenteen* magazine, "Basketball camp was fun."

19.) False: Justin, Lance, Joey, and Chris got the tattoos — not JC.

20.) True: Justin admits it in almost every interview he's ever done!

Multiple Choice

1.) (b) Lance Bass. Justin told *Live & Kicking* magazine, "My luggage got lost in New York. It came the next day, but I borrowed Lance's outfit anyway. He's a bit of a soft touch if I wanna borrow anything!"

2.) (c) Confidence. Justin told *Teen*, "Confidence is sexy to me. I don't like insecurity and jealousy."

3.) (b) Jason Sharp

4.) (d) www.rollingstone.com Justin told *People* magazine, "I check out rollingstone.com to see what the latest rumors are."

5.) (c) white. "My living room is all white, like something from that Lauryn Hill video for 'Ex-Factor,'" Justin told *Rolling Stone* magazine.

6.) (b) A water carrier

7.) (d) Biloxi at the Mississippi Coast Coliseum

8.) (a) Drew Barrymore

9.) (a) Professional basketball player. Justin told *Teen Beat*, "I'd love to play in the NBA . . . though I can't dunk!"

10.) (c) Two. It's true — he mentioned it in *Rolling Stone* magazine!

11.) (d) Eats ice cream. That's what he told the British magazine *Top of the Pops*, "Test ice cream," but then he added, "nothing helps except time."

12.) (d) Ryan Phillippe. [The hint was that Ryan is married to actress Reese Witherspoon!]

13.) (d) 4.8 million albums. 'N Sync, Britney Spears, and the Backstreet Boys are Jive's top-selling artists!

14.) (a) Kobe Bryant. At Jive's release party for *No Strings Attached*, Justin told *USA Today* columnist Jeannie Williams, "We decided all the musicians want to be basketball players and all the basketball players want to be musicians. So me and Kobe are going to trade places — after this year, he's going to join 'N Sync and I'm going to join the Lakers."

15.) (c) Lynn Harless. "I call my mom every day," Justin told *Teen* magazine when they were checking out his cell phone listings.

16.) (b) Videos of fans performing like 'N Sync. Justin told *Teen Beat* he absolutely loves it "when fans send us videos of themselves dancing to our music or mimicking us, acting like us."

17.) (d) The Oscars

18.) (c) Being late. Chris told *Smash Hits* magazine that the one thing that drives him crazy about Justin is "his tardiness — it always takes him a long time to get ready."

19.) (a) Joey Fatone, Jr. — Joey's birthday is January 28, 1977

20.) (d) Jonathan and Steven. The other 'N Sync siblings are: Molly, Kate, Emily, and Taylor — Chris; Tyler and Heather — JC; Stacey — Lance; Steven and Janine — Joey

21.) (b) Joey Fatone, Jr. He was an extra dancer on the show occasionally.

22.) (a) Bungee jumping — only once!

23.) (b) Christmas

24.) (a) Running around barefoot in his house. Justin told *Live & Kicking* magazine, "I miss that feeling when you walk into your own house and put your bare feet on to your carpet and it's, like, 'This is my carpet and I can run around if I want to.'"

25.) (c) Foot Locker: Justin has to check out the new sneakers!

26.) (d) Asparagus. Justin told *Twist* magazine, "I absolutely refuse to eat asparagus."

Mix & Match

1.)

(a) Joey Fatone, Jr.

(b) JC Chasez

(c) Chris Kirkpatrick

(d) Justin Timberlake

(e) Lance Bass

2.)

first — "I Want You Back"

second — "Tearin' Up My Heart"

third — "Merry Christmas, Happy Holidays"

fourth — "God Must Have Spent a Little More Time on You"

fifth — "Bye Bye Bye"

3.)

(c) Randall — Justin Timberlake; (b) Scott — JC Chasez; (e) Anthony — Joey Fatone, Jr.; (a)

Lance — Lance's full name is actually James Lance Bass; (d) Alan — Chris

4.)

(a) "Big Daddy" — JC Chasez

(b) "Scoop" — Lance Bass

(c) "Lucky" — Chris Kirkpatrick

(d) "Curly" — Justin Timberlake

(e) "Mr. Flirt" — Joey Fatone, Jr.